★GETTING TO KNOW★
SPAIN
and SPANISH

Written by
Janet De Saules

Illustrated by
Kim Woolley

BARRON'S

Contents

	Map of Spain	4
	Facts about Spain	6
	Regions of Spain	8
	Madrid	10
	In a typical Spanish town	12
	Eating in Spain	14
	What people do	16
	Children in Spain	18
	History of Spain	20
	Famous places	22
	Festivals	24
	Speaking Spanish	26
	At the café	28
	At the shops	30
	Index	32

First edition for the United States
published 1993 by Barron's Educational Series, Inc.

© copyright 1992 Times Four Publishing Ltd

First published in Great Britain in 1992 by
The Watts Group

All inquiries should be addressed to:
Barron's Educational Series, Inc.
250 Wireless Boulevard
Hauppauge, New York 11788

Library of Congress Catalog Card No.
92-38646

International Standard Book No.
0-8120-6339-2 (hardcover)
0-8120-1535-5 (paperback)

PRINTED IN BELGIUM

3456   9907   987654321

About this book

In this book you can find out about Spain — its people, landscapes, and language. For example, discover what the Spanish like to eat and drink, what they do for a living, and what famous Spanish places look like.

Where Spain is in the world

North America

South America

Europe

Africa

Asia

Australia

Find out, also, what school days are like for Spanish children, and about their vacations and festivals. On page 26, there is a special section to introduce you to speaking Spanish.

Hello!

¡Hola!

It explains how to use and pronounce everyday words and phrases, so you can make friends and ask for things in cafes and shops. Also, some Spanish words and their meanings are given throughout the book to help you increase you vocabulary.

Map of Spain

Spain is the second largest country in Western Europe. It has borders with France to the north, Portugal to the west, and Gibralter to the south.

The Spanish landscape is very beautiful and varied. There are high mountains in the north and south. The east and south coasts have long sunny beaches. In the center of the country, around Madrid, it is very hot in the summer, but the winters are cold.

Highest mountain: Teide Peak, Tenerife (Canary Islands), 12,198 feet (3,718 meters). This mountain is also an active volcano.

El Ferrol

La Coruña

Oviedo

Gijón

Cantabria

Asturias

Galicia

Cantabrian Mountains

Vigo

Castile-León

Valladolid

Sego

Salamanca

Sierra de Gredos

Portugal

Tagus

Extremadura

Guadiana

Sierra Morena

Guadalquivir

Córdoba

Seville

Andalusia

Málaga
Torremolinos

el país
country

Cádiz Marbella

Gibraltar (Br.

Strait of Gibraltar

Canary Islands

Tenerife

Lanzarote

Gran Canaria

4

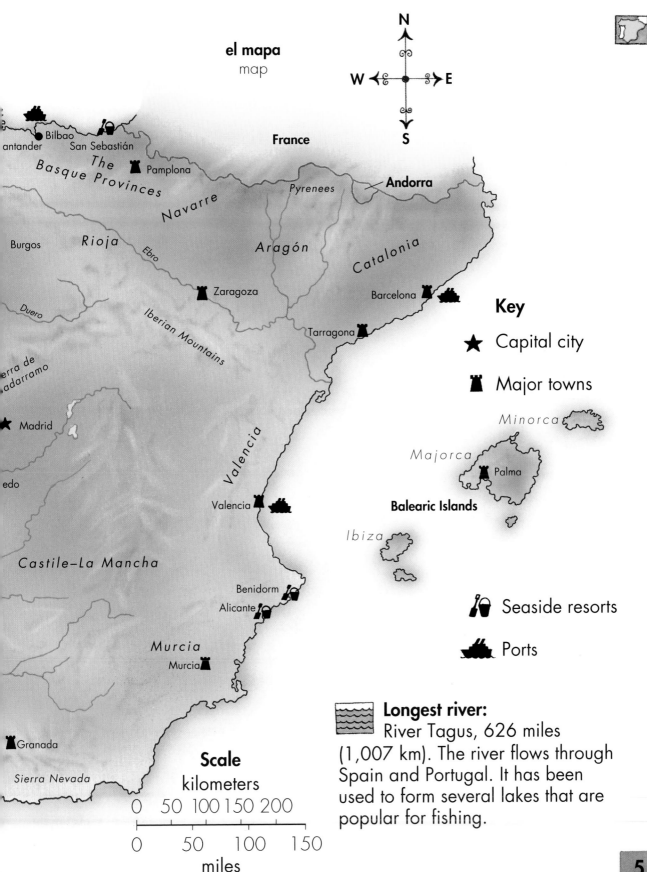

el mapa
map

N
W — E
S

Santander • Bilbao
San Sebastián

The Basque Provinces

Pamplona

Navarre

France

Pyrenees

Andorra

Burgos

Rioja

Ebro

Aragón

Catalonia

Duero

Zaragoza

Barcelona

Iberian Mountains

Tarragona

Sierra de Guadarrama

★ Madrid

edo

Valencia

Key

★ Capital city

♜ Major towns

Minorca

Majorca
Palma

Balearic Islands

Ibiza

Valencia

Castile–La Mancha

Benidorm

Alicante

🪣 Seaside resorts

🚢 Ports

Murcia

Murcia

Granada

Sierra Nevada

Scale
kilometers
0 50 100 150 200

0   50   100   150
miles
1 mile = 1.61 kilometers

Longest river:
River Tagus, 626 miles
(1,007 km). The river flows through
Spain and Portugal. It has been
used to form several lakes that are
popular for fishing.

5

Facts about Spain

Although Spain is about the size of Nevada and Utah together, almost 14 times as many people live there, so it is a much more crowded area.

 Size: 194,896 sq miles (504,783 sq km)

Population: 38,992,000

The Spanish flag looks a bit like a sandwich. It has a slice of red on the top and the bottom, and a yellow stripe in the middle.

la bandera
flag

In Spain the Head of State is the king. The king does not have much power, though. Important decisions about how the country is run are made by the prime minister and the government.

 Official name:
Espãna or **Estado Espãnol**
(State of Spain)

 Capital city:
Madrid

Language

Although nearly everyone can speak Spanish (known as **español** or Castilian), other regional languages are still spoken as well. The Spanish are very proud of all their languages.

In Catalonia, a region in the northeast, many people speak Catalan.

el lenguaje
language

Basque is spoken in the region where the north of Spain meets up with the southwest of France, called the Basque Country.

Galician is spoken in Galicia in the northwest.

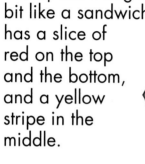

Money

Spanish money is the **peseta**. A small piece of candy costs about five pesetas.

el dinero
money

There are many different coins and bank notes. Coins are made in amounts of 1, 5, 10, 25, 50, 100, 200, and 500 pesetas.

Peseta notes are made in amounts of 1,000, 2,000, 5,000, and 10,000. Portraits of famous Spanish people are printed on the notes.

On the back of the notes the king's head is shown. Older coins have the head of General Franco, who ruled Spain from 1939 to 1975.

la moneda
coin

el billete de banco
bank note

Some things Spain is well known for

las naranjas
oranges
Valencia
Seville

los artículos de cuero
leather goods

el aceite de oliva
olive oil

el vino
wine
Rioja
Valdepeñas

el jerez
sherry

los coches
cars
Ford Fiesta, Ford Sierra

el turismo
tourism

Regions of Spain

Spain is divided into many regions. These include the Balearic Islands in the Mediterranean Sea, and the Canary Islands in the Atlantic Ocean, near the coast of Africa.

The Basque region in the north is sometimes called Green Spain as a lot of rain falls here all year round, making the land very fertile.

The northwest coast of Galicia is dotted with craggy inlets and old fishing villages.

San Sebastián and Santander are elegant seaside resorts on the north coast.

The center of Spain is boiling hot in the summer, but freezing cold in the winter.

Further south, the weather gets hotter and hotter and the land more and more dry.

Thousands of tourists from all over Europe spend their vacations at seaside resorts on the east coast. Benidorm on the Costa Blanca is one of the busiest.

el centro de turismo
resort

Further south along the east coast, orange groves surround the old city of Valencia. Among the groves are the farmers' small white-washed houses.

la casa
house

Rice is also grown in this region. Water from nearby rivers is used to flood the huge rice fields. With Valencia's warm climate, the rice grows quickly in the artificial lakes.

The southern region of Andalusia is the hottest and driest part of all Europe. On the coast, the Costa del Sol is very popular with vacationers. Wine is produced inland.

Some buildings in Andalusia look North African. This is because Spain was ruled by Arabs from North Africa for about 800 years.

Although Andalusia is very hot, the slopes of the Sierra Nevada are so high that people can ski there in winter.

Wild boar, wild goats, eagles, and vultures live in the mountains of the Pyrenees and southern Spain.

el ave
bird

The Canary Islands are covered with volcanoes. On the island of Lanzarote, the rocky landscape is very dramatic. Grapevines grow well in the black earth.

There are many national parks in Spain. Rare animals such as the Iberian mongoose and the Mediterranean lynx can be found to the south of Seville.

el animal
animal

Madrid

Madrid is Spain's capital city. It is situated in the middle of the country. More than three and a half million people live there.

Although the center of the city still has its old buildings, the outskirts are now crowded with huge modern blocks of apartments.

One of the most important buildings in Madrid is **El Museo del Prado**, an art gallery that contains many beautiful paintings.

There are many squares in Madrid. The main one is called the **Plaza Mayor**. People wander through here, or sit in the sun at one of the cafés. It is also used for plays and pageants.

Another big square is the **Plaza de España**. In the middle there is a statue of Don Quixote and Sancho Panza. The Spanish writer Cervantes, who invented these characters, died in Madrid in 1616.

Retiro Park was built by King Philip II. It has fountains, rose gardens, and a huge lake for boating.

Some famous sites

El Palacio Real
(Royal Palace)

Cibeles Fountain

La Puerta del Sol
(This is the center of the old city. There is a statue of a bear and a tree, which are the symbols of Madrid.)

Church of San Jerónimo
(where royal marriages take place)

La Puerta de Alcalá
(one of the city's gates)

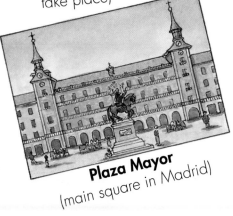

Plaza Mayor
(main square in Madrid)

Gran Vía
(major shopping street)

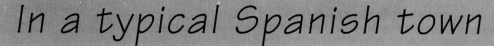

In a typical Spanish town

Most Spanish towns and villages are built around a square (la plaza). Here, people meet and sit in the sun.

As well as supermarkets, all Spanish towns have a market area where you can buy every sort of fresh food. They are busy places, full of life and noise.

la pastelería
pastry shop

la oficina de turismo
tourist office

el estanco
tobacconist

la panadería
bakery

el ayuntamiento
town hall

el banco
bank

la tienda de ultramarinos
grocery store

la ferretería
hardware store

la policía
police officer

Most people live in apartments. The furniture is often made of dark, polished wood. The Spanish like to have wooden or tiled floors to help keep their homes cool in the summer.

The church is an important part of every town. On Sundays, many families dress up and go to Mass in the morning.

Children often meet and play together in the town's square. In the evening, many families go out walking together. This is called **el paseo**.

la iglesia
church

la farmacia
pharmacy

el supermercado
supermarket

la papelería
stationers

la oficina de correos
post office

el quiosco
newspaper stand

Eating in Spain

The Spanish enjoy their food and they often eat out. At meals, family and friends can meet and talk about the day's events.

Breakfast **(el desayuno)** is very simple. Children might have a glass of warm milk and some cake or toast.

Halfway through the morning, people eat a sandwich or roll **(el bocadillo)**.

Some typical Spanish Dishes

Spain is famous for its **paella**. This is a colorful dish made with rice, saffron, and many types of seafood, such as lobster, shrimp, and mussels.

el gazpacho
tomato soup

los calamares
squid

la tortilla de patatas
omelette with potatoes

la fabada
thick bean and meat soup

Drink

el vino
wine
(Cava, Rioja, Valdepeñãs)

el jerez
sherry

la sangría
(made with red wine,
lemon and orange juice,
brandy, lemonade, and ice)

Bread is eaten with every meal. The main meal **(la comida)** is eaten between 2 P.M. and 3 P.M. The first course might be cold tomato soup **(el gazpacho)**, a salad, or vegetables. Fish or meat and French fries or salad are eaten as a second course.

For dessert, the Spanish like fresh fruit, custard **(flan)**, or ice cream.

la cerveza
beer
(San Miguel)

la horchata
(made from milk
and almonds)

el blanco y negro
(coffee with vanilla
ice cream on top)

el granzado
(fruit drink)

las tapas
tiny portions of food,
appetizers

la mortadela
slices of meat
with olives

el flan
custard

la tarta de manzana
apple pie

el chorizo
spicy sausage

What people do

Although there are many big industrial towns, much of Spain is still covered in countryside. Spain produces more food than many other European countries.

Olives are an important crop. They are grown all over Spain, except in the northwest. Spain exports more olive oil than any other country in the world.

la oveja
sheep

The merino sheep is raised in many parts of Spain. Its curly, silky fleece makes fine wool. Goats are grazed on the poorer land.

el granjero
farmer

The automobile industry employs more people in Spain than any other industry. Spain sells more cars abroad than any other west European country.

Farmers also grow wheat, barley, and rice. Oranges and tomatoes from the south and east are sold abroad. They bring a lot of money into the country.

el coche
car

Many people work in the fishing industry. Spain has the third largest fishing fleet in Europe. Fish is eaten all over the country, especially in Galicia.

el pescador
fisherman

la fábrica
factory

Coal, lead, copper, zinc, and mercury are mined. The mines employ many people.

Since the 1950s, Spain has become more and more industrialized. Large numbers of people have moved into the towns to look for work.

Many Spanish people work in factories that make things such as clothes, shoes, and other leather goods, cars, ceramics, chemicals, and computers.

Spain has more vineyards than anywhere else in the world. Wine and sherry are produced and sold all over the world.

la uva
grape

Bananas and grapes for wine are major crops on the Canary Islands. They are exported to other countries.

el plátano
banana

Even more people, though, work in the tourist industry. They work in bars and cafés, and in the huge hotels that have been built for vacationers along the sunny eastern and southern coasts.

17

Children in Spain

Here you can find out something about school days in Spain, and about how Spanish children spend their time.

 School in Spain starts early in the morning, and finishes around 5 P.M. There is a long break between 1 P.M. and 3 P.M. for lunch. Most children go home for this.

All Spanish children between the ages of 6 and 16 must go to school. After this, they can either leave and look for a job, or continue studying.

Most children go to schools that are free, run by the government. Other children go to private schools run by the Catholic Church, which the parents must pay for.

la escuela
school

los vestidos
clothes

Spanish children do not normally have to wear a uniform, so they can wear their own clothes to school.

We have two or three weeks of vacation at Christmas and one week at Easter.

We have 2 1/2 months off from school in the summer.

In June, the schools shut at lunchtime because it is too hot in the afternoon to have classes.

la piscina
swimming pool

During the school vacations, Spanish children spend a lot of time outside. They might go to meet their friends at a nearby swimming pool, or play soccer together.

el fútbol
soccer

Spanish children are allowed to stay up to watch television or play with their friends until very late. It is often after midnight when they go to bed.

las vacaciones
vacations

Most Spanish families still spend their vacations in Spain. In the summer, they may go to the seaside, or to the mountains to escape from the heat. In the winter, they may go skiing in the mountains.

During festivals, children dress up in the traditional costumes of their region. Many Spanish children learn **flamenco** dancing.

esquiar
skiing

los niños
children

History of Spain

Two thousand years ago Spain, like most of Europe, was part of the huge Roman Empire. These are some of the major events that have taken place since then:

A.D. 711

Muslim Arabs from the north of Africa invaded Spain. They took control of the country and ruled for almost 800 years. They built beautiful palaces such as the Alhambra in Granada.

1479

Ferdinand, the King of Spain, and his wife, Queen Isabella, set out to unite Spain against the Arabs.

1492

Finally, Ferdinand and Isabella's armies defeated the Arabs in Granada. The Arabs no longer had any power in Spain.

In the same year, Christopher Columbus discovered America for Ferdinand and Isabella. Spain began to colonize the New World. It also ruled the Netherlands and parts of Belgium and Italy. As a result, it became the richest and most powerful country in Europe.

el buque
ship

1588

Philip II of Spain tried to conquer England with a huge fleet of ships. His Spanish Armada was defeated, however, by Elizabeth I's forces.

1808

Spain was invaded by the French Emperor, Napoleon, who put his brother on the Spanish throne. The Spanish fought back, however, and the French were expelled.

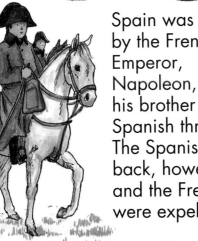

1931

The King of Spain was overthrown by the republicans and a new government was set up. This led to the Spanish Civil War.

1936–1975

In 1936, a Spanish general, Francisco Franco, rebelled against the republican government. Civil War broke out between his troops and supporters of the government.

One million Spaniards were killed in the Spanish Civil War. Franco won and went on to rule Spain as a dictator until 1975. Under his rule, Spain remained poor and cut off from the rest of Europe.

Now

Today democracy has been restored and Spain is a prosperous modern country. In 1986 it joined the European Economic Community.

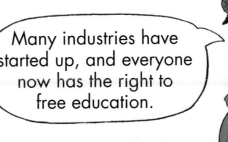

Many industries have started up, and everyone now has the right to free education.

Famous places

Every year, about 42 million tourists visit Spain. Many people from Britain, Germany, the Netherlands, and Scandinavia like to take their vacations along the hot and sunny Spanish coast.

Two of the most popular seaside resorts are Benidorm and Torremolinos on the Mediterranean coast. Benidorm was once a small fishing village. Today it is vast. Tall blocks of vacation apartments line the beaches, surrounded by bars, cafés, and discos.

la playa
beach

The coastline of the beautiful Balearic Islands has interesting caves to explore, as well as sandy beaches that are perfect for swimming and sunbathing.

> Most tourists visit Spain for the sea and sun, but there are many old and beautiful parts of the country to visit inland.

In the southern city of Granada is the palace of the Alhambra. It was built in the Arab style in the thirteenth and fourteenth centuries. The palace gardens are full of lakes and fountains.

One of the most famous buildings in Seville is the Giralda. This is a tower also built by the Arabs from north Africa (who were Muslims). Today it is part of Seville Cathedral.

la catedral
cathedral

Near Madrid is the ancient town of Toledo. Its ancient spired cathedral contains many paintings by the famous artist El Greco.

el palacio
palace

The artist, Picasso, lived in Barcelona for a time, and many of his paintings are kept there.

la pintura
painting

The royal palace of El Escorial is just outside Madrid. It is a huge stone building. It looks a bit like a castle from a frightening fairy tale. Inside are the graves of many of Spain's kings, queens, princes, and princesses.

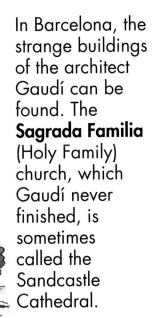

In Barcelona, the strange buildings of the architect Gaudí can be found. The **Sagrada Familia** (Holy Family) church, which Gaudí never finished, is sometimes called the Sandcastle Cathedral.

The ancient aqueduct of Segovia was built by the Romans in the first century A.D. It brought water from the Sierra Fonfría, 8 miles (14 km) away.

Summer is not the only season that is good for tourism. Many tourists enjoy the mild weather on the coast in the winter. Some go to the ski resorts in the mountains of the Sierra Nevada and the Pyrenees.

Festivals

Spanish holidays (fiestas) are a spectacular mixture of color, music, parades, costumes, and dancing. They take place throughout the year to celebrate various religious events. They might also be held to celebrate the beginning of spring, or the autumn harvest.

Romerías are picnic outings to a saint's shrine, held in country districts. People travel on horseback or in white covered wagons decorated with flowers. They sing and play guitars and castanets.

One of the most important fiestas is held in Seville during **Semana Santa** (Holy Week, the week before Easter). The people dress up in costumes decorated with semi-precious stones. Crucifixes and holy statues are carried on floats while sorrowful hymns are sung.

Seville's **Feria de abril** (April festival) is even noisier and more colorful than **Semana Santa**. Far into the night people sing and dance to **flamenco** music. Guitars and castanets are played. Many people wear traditional gypsy costumes.

el bailador
dancer

On the second Thursday after Whitsun, the festival of Corpus Christi is celebrated throughout Spain. The streets are covered in flowers, the town bells are rung, and there are noisy firework displays.

24

el modelo
model

In March, Valencia celebrates the **Fallas de San José**. Artists spend all year making huge paper-mâché models of people. These are painted with fantastic colors and put up in the squares or plazas all around the city.

los fuegos artificiales
fireworks

On the last night, the figures are burned on huge bonfires and fireworks are set off. The fire brigade has to make sure that the people and the nearby buildings are safe.

Many of Spain's festivals include bullfights. In some fiestas, the bulls run through the streets.

el toro
bull

At the San Fermín festival in the northern city of Pamplona, the people run with the bulls, trying to distract them with rolled-up newspapers.

Speaking Spanish

You will find lots of useful Spanish words on the following pages, plus some simple phrases to help you to ask for things.

Every word is written in three different ways:

these are the Spanish words

zumo de naranja
(THOOmo day narANha)
orange juice

this gives you an idea of how to pronounce the Spanish

this is what it means in English

In each speech bubble you will find a Spanish phrase, a guide to pronouncing it, and its English meaning. In the back of the book, you will find a Guide that will help you make the different Spanish sounds. The best way to practice is by saying the words aloud—if possible, to someone who knows how to pronounce them correctly.

the Spanish words

Quiero un pastel
(kee-AYro oon pasTEL)
I would like cake.

how to pronounce the Spanish words

the English translation

Making friends

Here are some simple Spanish phrases to use when you want to make friends.

Sí
(see)
Yes

Hola
(Ola)
Hello

Hola. ¿Cómo te llamas?
(Ola. KOmo tay YAmas?)
Hello. What is your name?

Me llamo María. ¿Y tu?
(may YAmo maREEa. ee too?)
My name is Mary. And yours?

No
(no)
No

Lo siento
(lo see-YENto)
I'm sorry

Por favor
(por faBOR)
Please

¿Dónde vives?
(DONday BEEbays?)
Where do you live?

Vivo allí.
(BEEbo a-YEE)
I live over there.

Señorita
(se-ny-orEEta)
Miss

Gracias
(GRAthee-as)
Thank you

Señor
(se-ny-OR)
Mr.

Adiós
(adee-OS)
Good-bye

¿Cuántos años tienes?
(KWANtos A-ny-os tee-AY-nays?)
How old are you?

Señora
(se-ny-ORa)
Mrs.

Perdone
(perDOnay)
Excuse me

Tengo doce años
(TENgo DOthay A-ny-os)
I am twelve.

¿Hablas inglés?
(ABlas eenGLES?)
Do you speak English?

At the café

un helado de fresa
(oon eLAdo day frAYsa)
strawberry ice cream

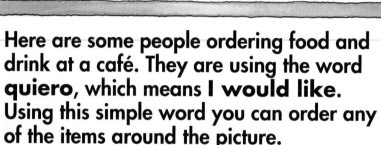
un zumo de manzana
(oon THOOmo day manTHAna)
apple juice

una jarra de agua
(OOna HAra day AGwa)
jug of water

la carta
(la KARta)
menu

Here are some people ordering food and drink at a café. They are using the word **quiero**, which means **I would like**. Using this simple word you can order any of the items around the picture.

¿Qué desean?
(kay daySAYan?)
What would you like?

un vaso
(oon BAso)
glass

Quiero un bocadillo de jamón y una limonada.
(kee-AYro oon bokaDEE-yo day haMON ee OOna leemoNAda)
I would like a ham sandwich and lemonade.

una ensalada
(OOna ensaLAda)
salad

camarero
(kamaRAY-ro)
waiter

una tarta de manzana
(OOna TARta day manTHAna)
apple pie

un helado de chocolate
(oon eLAdo day chokoLAtay)
chocolate ice cream

un bocadillo de queso
(oon bokaDEE-yo day KAYso)
cheese sandwich

un bocadillo de tortilla
(oon bokaDEE-yo day torTEE-ya)
omelette sandwich

Quiero un helado.
(kee-AYro oon eLAdo)
I would like ice cream.

¿De qué sabor – de fresa, de chocolate o de vainilla?
(day kay saBOR? day FRAYsa, day chokoLAtay o day ba-eeNEE-ya?)
What flavor—strawberry, chocolate, or vanilla?

¡Camarero! La cuenta, por favor.
(kamaRAYro! la KWENta, por faBOR)
Waiter! The bill, please.

la cuenta
(la KWENta)
bill

patatas fritas
(paTAtas FREEtas)
French fries

sal y pimienta
(sal ee peemee-ENta)
salt and pepper

camarera
(kamaRAYra)
waitress

un helado de vainilla
(oon eLAdo day ba-eeNEE-ya)
vanilla ice cream

aceite y vinagre
(a-THAYtay ee beeNAgray)
oil and vinegar

At the shops

la leche
(la LAYchay)
milk

el pan
(el pan)
bread

las galletas
(las ga-YAY-tas)
crackers

los huevos
(las WAY-bos)
eggs

la mermelada
(la mermayLAda)
jam

el coliflor
(el kolee-FLOR)
cauliflower

The children are shopping for fruit (fruta) and vegetables (legumbres) in a grocery store (tienda de ultramarinos).

¿Puedo ayudarle?
(PWAYdo a-yew-DARlay?)
Can I help you?

Sí, por favor. Quiero un kilo de manzanas.
(see, por faBOR. kee-AYro oon KEElo day manTHAnas.)
Yes, please. I would like one kilo (2 lbs) of apples.

el melocotón
(el maylo-koTON)
peach

las patatas
(las paTAtas)
potatoes

las peras
(las PAYras)
pears

un pollo
(oon POyo)
chicken

las salchichas
(las sal-CHEE-chas)
sausages

las gambas
(las GAMbas)
shrimp

Around the pictures are some useful words for things you might want to buy in other shops using the same phrase **Quiero.**

unos caramelos
(OOnos karaMELos)
candies

¿Cúantos quiere?
(KWANtos kee-AYray?)
How many would you like?.

Dos coliflores, por favor.
(dos kolee-FLOR-es, por faBOR.)
Two cauliflowers, please.

un pastel
(oon pasTEL)
cake

los sellos
(los SAY-yos)
stamps

un periódico
(oon payree-O-deeko)
newspaper

el tebeo
(el tayBAY-o)
comics

la crema para el sol
(la KRAYma PAra el sol)
suntan lotion

Index

 1 **dos** *(dos)* **3** **cuatro** *(KWATro)* **5** **seis** *(sayss)* **7** **ocho** *(O-cho)* **9** **diez** *(dee-AYTH)*

 uno *(OO-no)* **2** **tres** *(tress)* **4** **cinco** *(THIN-ko)* **6** **siete** *(see-AY-tay)* **8** **nueve** *(noo-AYbay)* **10**

enero *(enAYro)* January

 negro *(NEG-ro)* black

Alhambra, 20, 22
Andalusia, 9
Balearic Islands, 5, 22
Barcelona, 23
Basque Country, 6, 8
Benidorm, 8, 22
Bullfighting, 25
Canary Islands, 4, 9, 17
Catalonia, 6
Church of San Jerónimo, 11
Cibeles Fountain, 11
Columbus, Christopher, 20
Costa Blanca, 8
Drink, 15, 28
El Greco, 23
Escorial, El, 23
European Economic Community, 21
Farming, 16
Ferdinand, King, 20
Festivals, 19, 24
Fishing, 16
Flag, Spanish, 6
Flamenco, 24
Food, 14, 28–31
Franco, General, 7, 21
Galicia, 6, 8, 16
Gaudí, 23
Giralda, 22
Gran Via, 11
Granada, 20, 22
History, of Spain, 20
Industry, 16
Isabella, Queen, 20
La Puerta de Alcalá, 11

La Puerta de Sol, 11
Language, 6, 26–32
Madrid, 10
Money, 7
Museo del Prado, El, 10
Muslim Arabs, 9, 20, 22
Napoleon, 21
Palacio Real, El, 11
Pamplona, 25
Philip II, King, 10, 20
Picasso, 23
Plaza de España, 10
Plaza Mayor, 10
Population, 6
Produce, 7, 16
Pyrenees, 9, 23
Segrada Familia, 23
San Sebastian, 8
Santander, 8
School, 18
Segovia, 23
Seville, 22, 24
Shops, 12, 30
Sierra Nevada, 9, 23
Spain, map of, 4
Spanish Armada, 20
Spanish Civil War, 21
Sports, 19
Tagus, River, 5
Teide Peak, 4
Toledo, 23
Torremolinos, 22
Tourism, 17, 22
Valencia, 9, 25

 blanco *(blANko)* white

 febrero *(febRAYro)* February

 marzo *(MAR-tho)* March

 rojo *(RO-ho)* red

 abril *(ab-REEL)* April

 amarillo *(amaREE-yo)* yellow

 mayo *(MA-yo)* May

 verde *(BERday)* green

 azul *(a-THOOL)* blue

junio *(HOON-yo)* June

julio *(HOOL-yo)* July

 lunes *(LOOnays)* Monday

 agosto *(agO-sto)* August

 martes *(MARtays)* Tuesday

septiembre *(sept-YEM-bray)* September

jueves *(HWAY-bays)* Thursday

sábado *(SA-bado)* Saturday

diciembre *(deeth-YEM-bray)* December

miércoles *(mee-YER-kolays)* Wednesday

viernes *(bee-YERnays)* Friday

domingo *(doMINgo)* Sunday

noviembre *(nov-YEM-bray)* November

octubre *(okTOObray)* October